Miniskirts in The Waste Land

Pratibha Castle

First published 2023 by The Hedgehog Poetry Press

Published in the UK by
The Hedgehog Poetry Press
Coppack House, 5
Churchill Avenue
Clevedon
BS21 6QW

www.hedgehogpress.co.uk

ISBN: 978-1-913499-74-7

Contents

MINISKIRTS IN THE WASTE LAND

In a back street dive, a man in a baggy cardi
peddles Sal a tin of pills. Heading out, she
nicks a pack of Rider Waite *wicked cards*
checks them for propitious signs *speak to me*
the way all week she checks her knickers.

That term they read *The Waste Land*. Eliot's
words get her in the gut *them pills I took*
to bring it off. Opaque as trig, sixth form
sniggers *outside tit and second base* eavesdropped
in the locker rooms between hockey and maths.

Sister Bridget's caution, *occasion of sin.*
DJ's jokes on Radio Caroline. White noise.
Like the music listened to in bed
when she should have been asleep
but was trialling budding pleasure.

Next day, like a secret on a ripped-off page,
Sally slides a glance across the class
to Susie, seen last weekend loitering
outside the Palais by the Regal.

A bloke, *can't get no satisfaction,* old enough
to be her dad, greets Susie with a blasé barter
of saliva, steers her through the Palais door. Sally,
queuing for the late-night screening,
Girl on a Motorcycle, tugs her fringe, pops gum,
fidgets, keen to get down Faithfull's moves.

Sal's Biba skirt, two fingers below peril level,
baits the blush of lads on Vespas, engines
revving. Edgy for the crack of the starter's gun.

Summer's soundtrack *hurry up, it's time*
and televisions sizzle, shots of a Buddhist monk
ablaze, while Sally in a Surrey orchard contemplates
flesh, his and hers, pawed by fingers
in the fashion of Sassoon. Bare skin
tempted by a zephyr's careless brush, ripple grass, poppies
staining the yellowing stalks like spotting blood.

OCTOPUS RIDE

The cage dangles upside down
on the tip of a tentacle
flung, like a baby's arm,
to its steepest sprawl.

It idles in the breeze,
quivers, my knuckles white, tight
with clutching the metal bar.
A singe of sugar
rises from the candy floss stand

and axle grease, *Woolworth's* scent,
shouts, laughter, all the hurdy gurdy
grizzle of the fair.

I breathe
like sipping water
in a drought, barely enough
to keep me conscious lest,
falling into a belly bloating wail,
I loosen my grip.

How might it be
to slip, to soar, a swift
inscribing secrets,
or the blood clot
that might have been you
slipping out from between my legs,

to slump, akimbo, crooked star
glinting in the churned-up mud,
essence seeping
through its jelly fish skin.

REFLECTIONS

By the pond in Holland Park
a heron, herald
like the day down Portobello
sunlight, splintering a window,

dazzled, and my skirt,
a swirl of orange silk
and mirror discs, flashed
semaphore warnings I ignored.

In the market, costermongers' shouts
contused the air, gutters a carnage
of jaundiced cabbages, mossy lemons,
a tulip, crushed. You, kissing her,
beside *The Sun in Splendour.*

On the way home clouds, coffin-heavy,
silted the streets, stuttered traffic,
while in the bus halted next to mine
a girl wept my choked-back tears.

LIZZIE'S TRIP DOWN PORTOBELLO

Bodies eddy her along the street.
Through punters' chat. Costermongers
batting shouts like Epsom bookies.

By the Sally Army hall she halts.
Wishes Ernie would glance up
from tipping a bucket down the drain.
Shout *wotcha, gel.* Sidle her a wink.
An excuse to dawdle.
Relish sugar-scent of hyacinth.
Chance a haggle over a fist of freesias.

Ernie grunts, turns, greets the street.
Luverly daffs, ladies. Tanner a toss.

Corner of All Saints and Portobello,
women huddle. Hens
flocking. Pecking gossip.
Princess Margaret scarves
knotted tight as knuckles
beneath their chins.

If only Eulalia from the deli
would glance her way. Nod.
Elbow a chink into their cackling
congregation. Women's chat.
Absolution for a sin of solitude.
At murmurs of a poorly child,
Eulalia might dab an eye,
squeeze Lizzie's hand.

A woman in a red coat, rust hair
straggling through spider net, steel curlers,
billows smoke. Bandies her a glare
as if channelling Lizzie's thoughts.

Lizzie sighs. Ekes out cheer
of imaginary friendship. Drags her feet
like the terrier at the lamp-post
resisting its owner's tug.

At a bicycle chained to iron railings
beside a purple painted house,
she turns down worn steps
leading to the basement. A poppy
pushing through a crack
flutters, petal welcome.

The basement door creaks
open to a skank of damp.
She kicks it shut. The lock clicks.
Bolts out the dusk.

IN THE ATTIC

Tucked in the pocket
of an Afghan coat,
an anarchy of hankies,

Fox's glacier mint, ticket
to Regent's Park
for a long-ago rendezvous

with a man who failed to show
you glimpsed last week
in Holland Park, leaning

on a silver capped cane
his eyes no duller
than the morning

fifty years ago
down Portobello Road he
flourished a puce silk cravat

out from under spotted sheets
on a bric-à-brac stall beside
The Sun in Splendour. You

jealous of a girl he smiled at,
sitting on the kerb – bare feet
in the gutter, blue mould

orange, crumpled Rizla pack –
sipping on a reefer.
A henna-haired flower

in a cheesecloth frock
you itched to pluck, to crush.
The air a ferment

of patchouli, rotten apples.
Love the One You're With
coasting out an open window.

His maestro's hands that night,
white and fluent, charmed
you, all aquiver, from your lair

of convent niceties, and doubts.
Hexed with murmured phrases,
coaxing, till you pledged

to banish *Quelque Fleurs* and
Apple Blossom, douse yourself
in *Eau Sauvage,* suck mints.

MY SAVIOUR

Notting Hill, a bed-sit state
she'd fled to from the sticks
on leaving school. CND signs
scrawled on walls, graffiti
bleeding like the Jesus hearts
in all the convents she'd attended.
Long hair, bleary eyes, soul bro'
to the hippies in their purple flares, jellabas,
mumbling *wanna score?*

Landlady Aggie, largerthanlife poster
by her bed of Cynthia,
the naked biker-babe,
gossip hawked up
on a phlegmy Belfast cackle.
Lenient when the rent was late, a terror
to the drunken *gobshite* down the hall
who goosed her.

Dwayne, a Crosby 'tache,
butterfly patched jeans, Stetson,
finger pickin' starburst Gibson
cradled all the way from 'Frisco. Almost
tilting off the bed, off his head
on a pineapple fast, toke
of Acapulco Gold. 'Nam nightmares.

Laura Ashley floor-length frock,
stitched by candlelight
in a Maida Vale squat. She trips,
her cowboy boots spark flies
from black bags ditched by bin men
backing striking miners.

The day she kissed Dwayne's scars,
heard tales of paddy fields and
mortar brash as fireworks
watched on weed. The day
he curled her fingers
round a desert rose,
she hitched her dress,
joined him at the Registry,
made out, made up
harmonies to *I do.*

ARTICHOKES

They sprawl beneath an oak   drunk
on pheromones   honeysuckle whispers   skin tacky
with honeydew juices

noses cat-close   they
sip each other's breath
suck citrus the cut of cuticle moons
mango flesh

strip each other's selves
like plucking leaves
off artichokes

tongues   tender snakes
trace glistening lips
lick eye-lids   lobes
magic gully of a clavicle

murmur secrets   mime Hendrix riffs
hum Crosby Stills and Nash
Lark Ascending   declaim Cummings
...eyes big love crumbs

share munchies
chicken korma
chiku   lassi   fears

yield pomegranate seeds
garnet tears

kiss scars from the punch-up
in year nine   slide fingers
into mucky secrets

each peeled off self
more naked than the last
till what remains   squirms
worm-flush bare

WHEN I READ ABOUT THE WAR

I remember   your gun metal Beetle
chuntering down the Via Appia
a cough like my Singer treadle

the square off Piazza Navona
where we chilled
on a crumbling fountain edge
chaperoned by a pissing cherub
guzzled watermelon
pistachio ice
licked sugar trickles
off each other's chins
my milk skin curdling
in August blaze

I remember   stars
combusting in a cobalt sky
sand   and your gaze
burrowing in secret crevices
as we lazed   to heartbeat waves
octopus-limbed after loving
transported on the magic carpet
of your army sleeping bag

I remember   a siege
of pewter clouds
russet leaves
blitzing rubbish bags
outside my Chelsea flat
where I loitered in the hall
chewed split ends
watching for the post
your last note
smeary in my pocket
shipping out to 'Nam
tomorrow

I remember the day
an airmail like a moth
blue as your eyes
fluttered to the mat
green heroic script

Jeff mentioned you
This dude dropped by
Jeff's missing
Jeff's sister June

LEAVEN

Kneading dough, she hums
to Joni's *Ladies of the Canyon.*
Fashions loaves
to match her swollen belly.
Cossets an aching back.

Marvels at the mystery to come.
A tiny Buddha
who will tutor her
in spells, ocean ceilidh,
elegies of stones. Acorn tales
unfiltered as the vinegar
of apples seethed by bees.

A wonder she will bind
in scents of roses, milk,
a snowlace shawl
crocheted by a failing aunt
in fading black
with no-one
left to pamper.

Acolyte in a sisterhood
of mole-eyed girls,
she will tender
muslin, balm.
Little finger
tipped in honey
for a first sweet taste.

She taps crusts
as if entreating entrance
into a temple
to be blessed.
Feigns deafness

to siren fears of the unknown,
chuckles at a jumping bean
jab beneath her ribs.
Coaxes loaves
out of their tins
as if from cradles.
Murmurs 'come to me *mo chroí*'.

mo chroí [kree] my darling

THE QUICKENING

'wild queendom of Motherhood'
Liz Berry

Though you grew into a gravel-throated babe
whose 6'6" towers above my 5'2", my closet
cossets keepsakes from the time I 'crossed the border'
into the 'wild queendom of Motherhood'.

Silver teething ring, reminder of your mouth
gaping to attach to nipple or the knuckle
of a cooing visitor with no other
potable flesh to hand.

Nacreous tooth, cloth bunny – cross-stitch eyes –
interred under the bed with fluffballs
flourishing, no longer nourishing
the hoover, forlorn friend,
abandoned in the cupboard
beneath the stairs since my breakfast
became a bite of dry toast, slurp
of peppermint tea, upchuck scurry
to the loo. Dawn drill perfecting
the art of the fluidless heave.

Next came appetite like a starveling.
For some unfortunates it was sooty lumps of coal.
I was lucky. Fruit monkey, guzzling grapes
like bruised clots, luminous green popsicles, peaches
velvet-skinned, silkflesh nectarines. Bananas
freckled like old lady fingers. Satin
slither down the throat of avocado.

First suspicion of your presence, flutter
like a butterfly freed from its swaddling cocoon,
testing flight. In the bath, a V-shape
like Benbulben Mount – elbow? –
poking from my drumskin dune.

Penguinwaddle. Belly hefted out ahead
like a weight of hemp. Bebop
that had you boogying as I fingered a kaftan
in *Granny Takes A Trip*. Rugby buff
bumping my ribs in what? Size ten cleats.

Finale? Dragging pain familiar
from dress-rehearsal monthlies, nineteen hours,
climax of your seal slick body
on my chest, passport –
with a crown of sweat –
past the border
to my freaky queendom.

ST. JUDE OF THE LOST CAUSE

In the ambulance, I remember
how that time before
I pretended
this is little more
than the specs I'd lost one spring

when, dazed as the cat
who ate her kit,
I haunted the garden,
hoped to find them
by the yellow irises
encircling the pond,
in the compost bin

from which I'd spread
a comforter
of mulch
for the baby beetroot
swelling in the dark
like clotted blood,
their bruised leaves
having weathered
the rude tweaks
of sparrows.

Almost teatime at the hospital,
midwife Mary chirrups
it's a boy and you
are resting on my belly,
your blue gaze unblinking
as though taking stock,
searing me to the core, then,
before she snips
the lardy cord still linking us,
that's when I know
St Jude has come up trumps.

SEEKING *MOKSHA*

Known back home in Hove as Sue, Radha
renamed by a local guru,
opens the fridge on a rust of 'roaches.

They scrabble over one another's backs,
plunge from the rickety wire shelf
to certain death
yet – a miracle, it seems –
right themselves, scuttle
like dawn nightmares
down a crack in the wall.

Radha settles, cross-legged on a mat,
elephant god, joss sticks, rose quartz heart.
Chants AUM for world peace.

A rat hurtles through the door,
followed by a scrawny cat.
They skid, squealing,
beneath the bed.

Radha shrieks,
scrambles to her feet.
Ditches peace.

Krishna in a saggy nappy, hair
gold silk, spun by the sun,
staggers to his mother's side,
drops the papery skin of a snake
at her feet, heads back
to the bodhi tree, scrabbles in the trash,
crumpled bidi packs, orange peel,
jewel chikoo seeds
like flat black chestnuts.

Radha moans. Monkeys in the mango tree gibber, leap,
acrobat up leggy vines, pound the roof
of the crumbling villa, hill retreat
in a past life to a maharaja.
Incite a parrot's squawks.

Krishna coos, resurrects the green grin
rind of a watermelon, stops –
mid slurp – to pet a yellow dog
snuck in from the street
who licks the toddler's proffered bounty,
ogles as he takes another suck.

POSTCARD FROM GOA THAT I NEVER SENT

Parrots squawk matins, split the air
with emerald-scarlet swoops,
splatter Krishna's blue face.

Breeze wafts jasmine, wood smoke, scousers,
temple bells. A palm choked
with serpentine hibiscus
plonks a coconut
on the sand.

Back in Highgate, at *The Pig & Whistle,*
you are spewing rainy rhetoric,
spying out a clutch of chicks
for the next night's lay.

You stumble home alone,
under hangdog skies.

I gorge on mango moons. Flesh
seductive as kisses, lips
seasoned with a civet's shriek.
A gull's limp body dithers
in push-pull waves. Ocean mantra.
Ants chivvy a dead scorpion across my foot.

I torch your cast-off hat.

DOWN MAHATMA GANDHI ROAD

A river creeping like an oily snake.
Cracked-mud banks. Shanty town
of cardboard, string, corrugated roofs.
Prayer-plumes of smoke –
wood-fires, incense –
spiralling to Hanuman, to Shiva,
the sticks' dot tips, demons' eyes,
glinting in the night.

Refugee from rain,
you choke on diesel, dust,
rickshaws' rubber parps,
bicycle bells, scooters, shouts, tears
for a man who drove you
to this lemming flight.

Monkeys' rants, parrot's
yank you for a breath
out of your swampy self.
Mosquito whine, refrain
to the wheeze and jangle
of a squeeze box broadcast
over crackling speakers.
Slither of a woman's song.
Kohl bird's melancholy call
to its absent mate. Nimble smile
of a ragged child.

Faces. Ocean eyes. Swarming
at the fish-bowl windows
of your taxi, tetchy,
revving at the lights. Bodies
jostling, palms up-cupped,
contused with grime.
Baksheesh, baba, paese pae.
Heads jiggle. Gruel-shrill wails.
Wrists a bangle-clash of need.
Baby hungry, madam, paese pae.

Scurvy dogs
and goats
nose the limp corpses
of banana skins, orange rind.
Spices. Flesh. Drenching
jasmine breath. You,
amidst this pauper glut,
still lonely.

RAAT KI RANI (QUEEN OF THE NIGHT)

He beckons her to the bed
where his body curls,
a question mark,
on the scarlet quilt,
an invitation she accepts,
entering the current
of his caring as if into
Arabian Ocean spray
the way she dared
once, years ago,
under a Van Gogh sky,
bone-fingered stars
pushing peepholes
in asphyxiating night.

He draws her body
into his moulded form,
drapes an arm
weighty as peace
about her waist,
snugs her into his chest,
his sighs a lake
languid lapping
shores.

His fingers tangle
in her hair, gentle
yet firm enough
to reassure
I've got you babe,
you're safe now,
you can let go,
anchor her
before she tumbles
over crumbling
cliff-edge paranoia.

His whispers are a hive's forgiving hum
tipsy on jasmine, sea-fret
above a Candolim beach,

night soothed
by mantra of cicadas,
drenching moonflower scent, incense
genie charm of woman's laugh
rippling dark.

Raat ki Rani – night blooming jasmine

TO THE BEACH

A caravan of ants
escorts her along the track. It snakes
under mango trees,
past the whitewashed bungalow
of last night's party.
Palms snatch at light.
Banyans' aerial roots
grope shadows.

She pauses by a jasmine.
Sips scent of snow-star blossom.
A butterfly writhes
in spider mesh
on tongue-shaped leaves.
The goggle-eyed spinner
watches at the web's edge.

Breaking the threads,
she cradles the butterfly
in vaulted palms.
The creature flaps, stills
as she picks it free.
Blue wings
graze her skin,
an electric memory
of eyelashes
against her cheek.

A parrot squawks.
Kohl bird's wail
becomes her mother's song
soaring above smoke
coiling from an altar boy's censor.

The breeze falls.
Jungle voices fade,
and her jangled thoughts.
Heart-beat waves
sigh beyond the trees.

ACKNOWLEDGEMENTS

My thanks to the editors of the following publications, where some of these poems were first published, sometimes in different versions: *Agenda, Alchemy Spoon, Dreich, International Times, Live Encounters, Orbis, Poetry and All That Jazz, Reach.* Poems have been commended, highly commended or longlisted in the following competitions: Binsted Arts, Indigo Press, Bridport Prize. Poems have been read at the Cheltenham Poetry, and Gloucestershire Poetry Festivals, with thanks to Anna Saunders and Josephine Lay respectively. Also Pig Hog Brighton, Chichester Open Mic, Cultivating Voices Live, The Poetry Place: West Wilts Radio, Woking Write Out Loud, Arundel Arts Junction, Torriano House, Like A Blot From The Blue, Poets Prattlers and Pandemonialists, Offa's Press Virtual Voices, with thanks to Michaela Ridgway, Barry Smith, Sandy Yannone, Dawn Gorman, Greg Freeman, Mike Carey, Pauline Seward, Fin Hall, Emma Purshouse, and Stephen Fletcher.

Naomi Foyle's insight and mentoring has helped to bring this pamphlet to fruition, along with encouragement, as ever, from Simon Jenner. Many poets have helped with feedback through multiple drafts: Camilla Lambert, Clair Chilvers, Jacqueline Schaalje, and in particular Chris Hardy; members of the Chichester Stanza group, SKEGS, and Retreat to Advance.

I am grateful to Mark Davidson of Hedgehog Poetry Press for his faith in my poetry as well as his ongoing help and support. If I have overlooked anyone's help and kindness, please forgive me. Know it is down to the ravages of the passing years, and not a lack of appreciation.

And a final, heartfelt gratitude to my husband and son for their unending support, encouragement and love.